爱护我们的地球

Sharing the Planet | Non-Fiction Series

Copyright © 2022 by Level Learning, INC. and Washington Yu Ying PCS™
Original and Edited Text Copyright © 2022 by Washington Yu Ying PCS™

All rights reserved. No part of this book in whole or part may be reproduced without written permission from the publisher.

Published by Level Learning, INC.

Content Contributors:
Washington Yu Ying PCS™ - Qianyi (Shirley) Zhang, Pearl Zao He You
Level Learning - Jingyao Qi

Illustrations by: Josh Taira

Leveling classification based on Level Learning standard.
For full description, visit www.levellearning.com

ISBN 978-1-64040-058-0
Simplified Chinese Edition

About Level Learning:
Level Learning provides a literacy focused curriculum specifically designed for K-12 Chinese as a Second Language classrooms. Our program offers 20 levels of specific and detailed objectives, leveled texts and passages, mastery-based online assessment, and analytics to enable data-driven instruction. Level Learning reading curriculum for both literature and informational text emphasize grammar and comprehension skills to help teachers develop confident and independent Chinese language readers. The non-fiction series of books are specifically designed to support our informational text course based on multiple national standards. To learn more about our entire offering, visit www.levellearning.com.

About Washington Yu Ying PCS™:
Washington Yu Ying PCS is a Mandarin English dual language immersion International Baccalaureate (IB) World school. Yu Ying's mission is to inspire and prepare young people to create a better world by challenging them to reach their full potential in a nurturing Chinese/English educational environment. Yu Ying's comprehensive IB, dual immersion curriculum equips students with global competencies for success in the real world. As a leader in immersion education, Yu Ying is determined to advance Chinese language programs and global citizenry education by helping other schools create and strengthen their Chinese programs. For more information, email: products@washingtonyuying.org

人们的生活离不开空气、水、食物和能源。可是环境污染和能源浪费却每天都在发生着。

污染主要是一些有害的垃圾引起的。这些垃圾可能是人们每天的生活垃圾，可能是工业垃圾，也可能是农业垃圾等等。

如果有害的固体垃圾进入泥土中,农作物就会被污染;有害的液体垃圾流入河里,水源就会被污染;有害的气体垃圾飘到空中,空气就会被污染。

这些污染都会危害人们的健康。我们要怎样减少污染和浪费呢?

第一，我们可以多使用可回收或可分解的生活用品。这样就会减少有害的固体垃圾。第二，我们可以节约用电。要知道，发电厂是制造液体垃圾最多的工厂之一。减少用电就会减少水源污染。

第三，我们可以少开车，多骑自行车或乘坐公共交通工具。这样就会减少空气污染。第四，我们可以节约用水。刷牙的时候，要记得把水关掉，把雨水存起来浇花，不要长时间洗澡等。

另外,我们也可以多种树,把家里的垃圾分类,减少使用塑料制品,不浪费食物等。这些事,看起来都是小事情,可是都会帮助我们减少污染,减少浪费。

地球是我们的家园。爱护地球,从每一个人做起,从每一件小事做起。

Glossary

	Pinyin	English Definition
空气	kōng qì	air
能源	néng yuán	energy, power source
环境	huán jìng	environment
污染	wū rǎn	pollution
浪费	làng fèi	to waste
害	hài	harm
垃圾	lā jī	waste
工业	gōng yè	industry
农业	nóng yè	farming, agriculture
固体	gù tǐ	solid
农作物	nóng zuò wù	crop
液体	yè tǐ	fluid
水源	shuǐ yuán	water supply
气体	qì tǐ	gas
飘	piāo	to float

	Pinyin	English Definition
危害	wēi hài	to harm
减少	jiǎn shǎo	to reduce
使用	shǐ yòng	to use
回收	huí shōu	recycle
分解	fēn jiě	decompose
用品	yòng pǐn	products
节约	jié yuē	to conserve
电	diàn	electricity
发电厂	fā diàn chǎng	power plant
制造	zhì zào	to make, to manufacture
工厂	gōng chǎng	factory
骑	qí	to ride
自行车	zì xíng chē	bicycle
公共	gōng gòng	public
交通工具	jiāo tōng gōng jù	transportation

Glossary

	Pinyin	English Definition
刷牙	shuā yá	to brush teeth
关掉	guān diào	to turn off
存	cún	to save
浇花	jiāo huā	to water plants
分类	fēn lèi	to sort
塑料	sù liào	plastics
地球	dì qiú	earth
家园	jiā yuán	homeland
爱护	ài hù	care

www.ingramcontent.com/pod-product-compliance
Lightning Source LLC
Chambersburg PA
CBHW041223070526
44584CB00001B/70